CIGARS

RED HOWARD

MetroBooks

To my mom for planting the seed, to Steve Wolf for helping me roll, and to my wife Kathryn for igniting the flame.

MetroBooks
An Imprint of Michael J. Friedman/Fairfax Publishers

Published in 1997 by Michael Friedman Publishing Group, Inc. by arrangement with Todtri Productions Ltd.

Copyright © 1997 by Todtri Productions Limited.

Library of Congress Cataloging-in-Publication data available upon request.
ISBN 1-56799-603-5

This book was designed and produced by
Todtri Productions Limited
P.O. Box 572, New York, NY 10116-0572
FAX: (212) 279-1241

Author: Red Howard

Publisher: Robert M. Tod
Editorial Director: Elizabeth Loonan
Senior Editor: Cynthia Sternau
Project Editor: Ann Kirby
Photo Editors: Heather Weigel, Meiers Tambeau
Production Coordinator: Jay Weiser
Designer: Kathryn Siegler

Printed and bound in Singapore

For bulk purchases and special sales, please contact:
Friedman/Fairfax Publishers
Attention: Sales Department
15 West 26th Street
New York, NY 10010
212/685-6610 FAX 212/685-1307

Visit our website:
http://www.metrobooks.com

PICTURE CREDITS:

Art Resource, New York
Tate Gallery, London 17
National Museum of American Art, Washington D.C. 64–65, 113; Jewish Museum, New York 66
Bridgeman Art Gallery, London 73
Musée Toulouse-Lautrec, Albi 100

D. Blümchen & Company, Inc. 7 (top right), 37 (bottom left & bottom right), 41 (top left), 42 (top right), 44 (bottom right), 50 (top right), 56 (top right & bottom left), 101 (bottom right), 107

Bulgari Corporation of America 99 (top right)

Cigar Aficionado 67 (top & bottom left), 91 (top)

Cigar Connection 22, 32

Colibri 104 (top & bottom)

Corbis–Bettmann 6 (bottom right), 9 (top), 10 (top), 11 (top & bottom), 12–13, 16 (bottom), 27, 28 (top & bottom), 29, 30, 34, 36, 43, 46–47, 48, 49, 53 (top left & bottom right), 57, 62 (bottom), 78 (bottom), 84, 85, 86–87, 89 (top), 96, 97, 106, 115

Sally R. Daly 70

Cuba Club, Miami 76 (top)

Culver Pictures 15 (bottom), 21 (bottom), 24–25, 54 (top right)

Davidoff of Geneva (CT) Inc. 93, 112 (bottom right)

Daniel Douke 63

David W. Dyson, England 109

Tabacalera A. Fuente y Cia 76 (bottom), 77 (bottom), 94 (top), 99 (bottom left)

Abby Gennet 5

Jacques Halbert 60, 75

Hollco Rohr 21 (top)

The Kobal Collection 38–39, 50 (bottom left), 51, 52, 80

Laurence Leblang Creative Services 7 (bottom right), 59 (bottom left)

Mayor's Jewelry/deBoulle 114

Kim McCarty 8

M & N Cigar 110–111

Modernism Gallery 4, 71

Susan Patricola Public Relations, Inc. 77 (top), 98

Photofest 88, 91 (bottom)

Richard Pierce 92

Richard Polsky Works of Art, San Francisco 63

Private Collections
Rick and Dana Dirickson 63
Christopher J. Howard 99 (bottom right)
Todtri Productions 9 (bottom)

Antonio M. Rosario 15 (top), 33, 44 (top left), 58, 74 (top & bottom right), 81 (bottom), 90 (top), 95, 99 (bottom right), 102–103, 105, 112 (top left & bottom left), 116, 118, 119, 120, 121, 122, 123, 124, 125

Shooting Star 40 (top right), 41 (bottom right), 42 (bottom right), 45, 53 (bottom left)
Yoram Kahuna 79
Michael Virden 83

Stanley Kolker & Associates, Inc. 16 (top), 76 (bottom), 77 (bottom), 94 (top), 99 (bottom left)

Jerry Striker 6 (top & left), 7 (top left), 9, 10 (bottom left), 18–19, 20 (bottom), 35, 37 (top right), 54 (bottom left), 55, 56 (bottom), 59 (top right), 101 (top right & bottom left)

Sygma Photo News
Ted Soqui 90 (bottom)

Bill Terry 23

Vorhaus & Company 108 (top & bottom), 110–111

Ed Weigel 70

Kenneth M. Wyner 68

Special thanks to Sandra Aldana of The Cuba Club; G.R. Barron & Company; D. Blümchen & Company, Inc.; Bulgari Corporation; *Cigar Aficionado*; Cigar Connection; Colibri; Consolidated Cigar Corporation; Domenic Corbo of Smokin' Sounds; Sally R. Daly; Davidoff; deBoulle; David W. Dyson; Paul Garmirian; Marshall Gordon; Havana Tea Room and Cigar House; Hollco Rohr; Christopher J. Howard; Stanley Kolker; Lane Limited; M & N Cigar; Mayor's Jewelry; Kim McCarty; Miami Cigar; Michael's Restaurant; Marco Miguel Tobacco Corporation; Modernism Gallery; Mom's Cigar; Susan Patricola; Richard Polsky; Antonio M. Rosario; Nat Sherman; *Smoke* Magazine; Jerry Striker; Topper Cigars; Vorhaus & Company

CONTENTS

INTRODUCTION

"There is nothing more agreeable than having a place where one can throw on the floor as many cigar butts as one pleases."

—FIDEL CASTRO

*I*t's been a pretty long day. Maybe it was the office, maybe it was the weather, maybe it was some jerk on the freeway. But you've made it—you've survived another day in the jungle to arrive home and relax. You peel off the beige monkey suit, feeling a little more at home with each layer you shed. You relax with a bite to eat, wearily looking over the day's mail; you decide it can wait. The telephone rings, screaming for your attention; you decide that can wait, too. With the warmth of darkness settling in around you, you pour yourself a cold one and kick back. To this delicious concoction you add one more piece to the puzzle: a fine cigar. As you delight to the first crackling sounds of flame hitting cigar, you take a long, luxurious puff on a favorite brand and you melt. You simply melt.

What is it about a fine cigar that makes you feel so good when you felt so lousy? Cigars have always added up to a delicious sum of relaxation and comfort. But aren't they just a bunch of dried up leaves? Hardly. From the earliest Indian smokers of North America to the young turks of the New York modern cigar bars, cigars have held a mystique that transcends the tobacco inside them— their visceral appeal is as intangible as the smoke they produce, yet every bit as present.

But to say that a cigar is just a symbol of leisure is to ignore the immense pride that goes into making a

Left: Martini with Havana Punch, Guy Diehl, 1995. Acrylic on canvas, 14 x 16 in. (35.5 x 40.5 cm).

*"The cigar numbs sorrow and fills the solitary hours with a
million gracious images"*

—GEORGE SAND

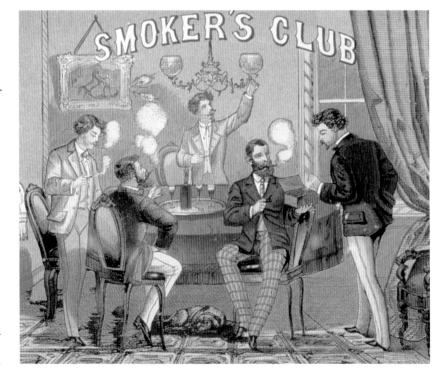

cigar. Let's face it, it's not that easy to make a quality smoke. Think
about this the next time you torch a Punch, or cut the end of a La
Gloria Cubana. Every cigar is more than just tobacco: It's a piece of
art, a veritable statue constructed by some of the finest artists in the
world, artists that have learned their craft from their parents, who
learned their craft from their parents, and so on.

Cigars are more than just a business, they're a dynasty. At the heart of this dynasty
is a relationship that spans a thousand miles, crossing complex political and geographical
boundaries; it's the relationship between roller
and smoker, two people who don't know anything about one another, and who would
never meet in a million years. It's as if the
magic of cigars has spanned a vast stretch of
time, distance, and culture to bring together
these two individuals for a common purpose.
The roller applies great skill and tradition to
his art, knowing this precision will make for a
world-class smoke; the smoker approaches the
smoke with reverence for the maker's skill, and
an appreciation for the product. It could be a
cigar maker in Havana, and a bread maker in
Hoboken—it doesn't matter.

Not since the turn of the century, when cigar
smoking was at its height, have cigars been

such a hit. At that time, a cigar was a fixture in the lives of every American male. Not a luxurious pastime, but an article of everyday life, and as much a part of one's outfit as a pair of shoes or a hat. I dare you to find a middle-aged American who doesn't remember their grandfather smoking a cigar. The intervening years, however, have not been so kind to the big smoke. The U.S. trade embargo with Cuba and the health issues surrounding the smoking of cigarettes are just two events that have taken the cigar from the staple of the home to the bastion of the backyard. Banned from society, the cigar smoker became the guy who smelled bad.

Then, seemingly out of nowhere, the cigar returned, but with a different spin. No longer the accessory of the masses, the cigar is now the plaything of the discerning. Mass produced, machine-made cigars are out, premium hand-rolled varieties are in. And to everyone's relief, women are taking an equal part in this celebration of smoke, lending a much needed gender balance to this traditionally all-male sport.

We can pinpoint many factors for this resurgence, from the emergence of *Cigar Aficionado* magazine in September 1992, to the accumulation of wealth that came from the baby boomers' generation reaching their peak earning years. Whatever. The point is, cigars are back, and with them is a newfound appreciation of the skill, patience, and attention that cigar manufacturing requires.

With this, we return to our deflated office rat, finishing off the day with a fine cigar. Is he immediately aware of the months, even years, this tobacco sat aging in factories? Does he stop to think about the hundreds of times some guy in Honduras had to check on the tobacco plant that made his cigar's wrapper? I doubt it. But when a fine cigar works its meditative magic over a mere mortal trying to get through the day, do you think he senses the care and nurturing that went into his fine smoke? You bet.

Left: Smoker's Club, by G. S. Harris and Son.

You Talking to Me?, Kim McCarty, 1991. Oil on canvas, 60 x 48 in. (152.5 x 122 cm).

CHAPTER ONE

CIGAR HISTORY, GROWING, AND MANUFACTURING

*T*he history of the cigar is generally regarded to have started with Columbus. It was shortly after his historic landing in 1492 that Columbus set his sails south and stumbled onto Cuba, where he was greeted by natives smoking a roll of dried leaves. Though not a big smoker himself, Columbus nonetheless brought this newfound delicacy back to Spain and started that country's exclusive three-hundred-year love of cigars. In fact, the word "tobacco" is considered to be derived from the "tobago" or "tobaca," a hollowed piece of cane used by West Indian natives to inhale finely powdered tobacco.

It wasn't until the eighteenth century that cigar smoking began to spread to the rest of Europe: first to France, and then to Holland and Russia. The word "nicotine" is actually named after the French ambassador to Portugal at the time, Jean Nicot. It was during this time that the first cigar band was seen. Although the Germans (who perfected printing technologies) are often credited with the cigar band, it was actually the Russian Empress Catherine II who insisted that her cigars be made with bands made of silk, lest her royal fingers be stained by tobacco.

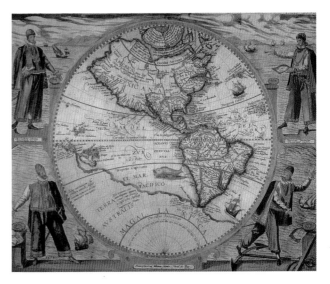

The cigar made its first appearance in America in 1762, when Colonel Israel Putnam introduced the

A regal cigar foe. *Portrait of Queen Victoria* (1819–1901) by Winterhalter, 1837.

colonies to this new way of enjoying tobacco. Putnam, a British officer back from war in Cuba, returned to Connecticut with a supply of Cuban leaves, thus perpetuating a long history that region had with tobacco. To this day, Connecticut has been the focal point of America's domestic cigar tobacco cultivation, and the Connecticut wrapper leaf is considered one of the finest outside of Cuba.

By the early nineteenth century, cigar production had begun to take off in America. However, since snuff and the clay pipe were the more popular ways to "take" tobacco, it would be some years until the custom would take hold. Meanwhile, in Europe, Spain's King Ferdinand VII was expanding tobacco production in Cuba, then a Spanish colony. The stifling customs of the Victorian age notwithstanding, cigars generally grew in acceptance in nineteenth-century Europe, culminating with the introduction of the smoking jacket in France in the latter part of the century.

In England, the cigar (and all tobacco for that matter) had an ardent foe in Queen Victoria. Her hatred of the habit gave rise to the smoking room, since taking tobacco in public was highly frowned upon. However, her son and heir to the English throne, Edward, Prince of Whales, was an adamant cigar smoker. In 1901, the newly coronated King Edward royally proclaimed, "Gentleman, you may smoke!" With this single line, King Edward became synonymous with cigars, and the cigar bearing his name was one of the most popular cigars manufactured during the first part of this century.

Cigars hit big in the United States at the turn of the twentieth century, at which time cigar sales hit an all-time high, surpassing even today's lofty numbers. Domestic production increased rapidly, although there was still a marked distinction between cigars made with domestic tobacco and those made with all-Havana tobacco, which were called "clears." The main difference was the price, with a Cuban cigar costing up to a hefty twenty cents. In 1919, this caused Vice President Thomas Marshall, to utter the famous words, "What this country really needs is a good five-cent cigar." This five-cent cigar became a reality by the 1950s as the

Fidel Castro
lights up in
Cuba, 1963.

machine roller made less expensive cigars from America, and even Cuba, widely available.

With Fidel Castro assuming power in the 1959 Cuban revolution, the writing was on the wall for American lovers of Cuban cigars. In 1962, U.S. President John F. Kennedy signed the Cuban trade embargo, and all U.S. imports of Cuban cigars and cigar tobacco screeched to a halt. U.S. manufacturers stockpiled Cuban tobacco and it was still possible to get a cigar made of Cuban tobacco into the 1970s. Today, much of the cigar production for the United States is being done in Cuba's neighboring countries, mainly Honduras, Jamaica, and the Dominican Republic. In some cases, these regions produce cigars with the same brand names as popular Cuban makes, since many companies (and the families that owned them) split after the embargo. The result? Confusion all around. For example, both Cuban and Honduran Hoyo de Monterreys are sold in Europe.

A TOTAL EMBARGO, SORT OF . . .

JFK's press
secretary and
cigar delivery
man, Pierre
Salinger.

In 1961, President John F. Kennedy decided that he had enough of Fidel Castro's band of merry communists having the run of the joint in Cuba, so he decided to impose a total trade embargo with the country, an economic blockade that continues today. But there was one hitch: Kennedy was a big fan of Cuban cigars. Not to be left out in the cold without his beloved smoke, Kennedy called his press secretary, Pierre Salinger, into his office and told him to find one thousand H. Upmann Petit Coronas immediately. When asked why, Kennedy hesitated. Salinger was told to do it without question.

After a frantic search of the Washington area, Salinger returned the next day with almost twelve hundred of the Upmann cigars. Kennedy inspected his new stash, then reached into his pocket and handed Salinger a piece of paper, telling him to call a press conference. Salinger opened the paper to find it included a presidential decree ordering a total trade embargo with Cuba. A stunned Salinger left the office, and made the announcement. Later, Kennedy was to continue his enjoyment of Cuban cigars despite the embargo. JFK would have his close friend, British Ambassador David Ormsby Gore, smuggle Cubans into the White House from London. While the embargo on Cuban cigars endured, Kennedy remained well-stocked.

President Kennedy takes a break from the action and lights up aboard the Aircraft Carrier *Kitty Hawk*, 1963.

Sorting, Packing and Banding Cigars at the factory of SANCHEZ & HAYA COMPANY, makers of the Finest Havana Cigars, Factory No. 1, Tampa, Florida.

CIGAR GROWING AND MAKING

The next time you light up a fine cigar, stop for a second and think about what goes into making one. The entire cigar-making process, from the growing of tobacco, to its drying, aging and fermentation, and finally to its rolling, all have one thing in com-

mon: work. Making cigars is a very labor-intensive process, and takes a ton of time. But this makes sense. Nothing this fine has ever come out of a machine, and never will. Sure, there are machine-made cigars: Many of the brands you find in your cor-

ner liquor store are not rolled by hand. Before a tobacco leaf is made into one of the world's best brands, it will be handled and inspected thousands of times, in a very long and arduous process that can only be avoided by lessening the quality of the cigar. For the best cigar makers in the world, this is simply not an option.

Where The Cigars Are: Growing Regions

Cuba. It goes without saying that Cuba is the most famous cigar growing region in the world. Cuban cigars have always been the most popular and most sought-after cigars. However, the devastating one-two punch of the American embargo and the elimination of support from the Soviet Union has severely curtailed the ability for this small Caribbean country to produce tobacco. Exports of Cuban cigars, topping $100 million in the early eighties, are half of that now. But high prices and charges by connoisseurs that Cuban cigar quality has dropped have done little to tarnish the allure of the Cuban cigar, especially to the American smoker who still eyes a Cuban cigar as a forbidden fruit. Rich and fertile soil, optimum climate, and abundant rainfall makes the Pinar del Río province in western Cuba the world's premier cigar growing region.

Honduras. Honduras is the one of the largest producers of premium cigars, second only to Cuba. In the past, much of this country's tobacco growing efforts have been frustrated by the ongoing wars in neighboring Nicaragua. But in the 1990s, Honduras has emerged as a serious competitor to Cuba for the cigar crown. Many prominent cigar makers settled there after the Cuban embargo, and U.S. imports of Honduran premium cigars jumped from 100 million to 140 million in just three years.

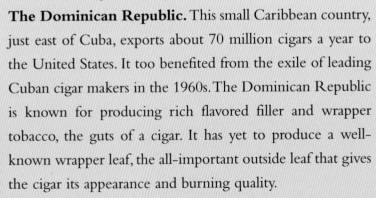

The Dominican Republic. This small Caribbean country, just east of Cuba, exports about 70 million cigars a year to the United States. It too benefited from the exile of leading Cuban cigar makers in the 1960s. The Dominican Republic is known for producing rich flavored filler and wrapper tobacco, the guts of a cigar. It has yet to produce a well-known wrapper leaf, the all-important outside leaf that gives the cigar its appearance and burning quality.

Connecticut. In the long tradition of east coast tobacco plantations, Connecticut has emerged as a source of premier wrapper leaves. The uniquely sandy soil of this state produces the Connecticut Shade, one of the most expensive tobacco leaves in the industry.

Topper Cigars
with Connecticut
broadleaf
tobacco wrapper.

GROWING AND HARVESTING

The long journey from leaf to cigar starts with a seed in the earth. A tobacco farmer will spend the long, hot months of summer working the soil of his plantation, or *vega*. Cigar tobacco demands the loosest possible soil, and to make ready for the coming harvest, the land is plowed many times.

Starting in October, seeds are planted in stages to ensure that there is adequate labor available for harvest. Seeds are planted on level fields, so that they will not be washed away, and are covered with straw or cloth to promote germination. In Cuba, seeds are provided free of charge by Tobacco Research Stations. Thirty to forty-five days after planting, the seedlings become six to eight inches (fifteen to twenty centimeters) high and are ready for planting.

Once the seedlings are transplanted, they will take forty-five to fifty days to reach maturity. During this time, the plant will be inspected hundreds of times for pest prevention and pruning. As the plant grows, flower buds and side shoots are removed.

Carlos Fuente—father and son—looking over their crop in the Dominican Republic.

Delicate wrapper leaves are grown under a muslin cloth covering, or *tapado*.

The delicate leaves that make up the all-important wrapper (or outside of the cigar) come from the corojo plant, which gives the cigar its appearance and burning quality. A corojo plant is grown under a covering, or *tapado,* made of muslin cloth to protect it from the sun, which can cause the leaves to get too dense for use as wrappers. It will take about forty days for a corojo plant to be ready for harvest, at which time it will yield eight or nine pairs of leaves.

Asher Wertheimer,
John Singer
Sargent, 1898.
Tate Gallery,
London, Great
Britain.

The criollo plant yields a variety of different leaves that are blended for the filler, or inside of the cigar, and the binder, the less critical inner wrapper that holds the filler together. Together with the wrapper, the binder and filler make up the three different parts of a cigar. Unlike the corojo plant, the criollo plant is exposed to full sun, which creates a greater variation in the types of leaves produced. The top of the plant produces leaves that are very rich in flavor, whereas the bottom leaves are denser and better suited for filler tobacco which affects the way a cigar burns. It's the way that these different types of tobacco leaves are blended together that gives each cigar its unique taste. Specific blends are carefully guarded secrets among cigar manufacturers.

The harvest begins in January. The plants, now approximately fifty days old, are picked by hand. To be sure that leaves are picked at precisely the right moment, each plant is visited repeatedly over a forty-day period, with only two or three leaves picked each time. A very precise and time consuming task, to be sure.

ANATOMY OF A TOBACCO PLANT

A single tobacco plant can produce a variety of different types of leaves. Depending on where the leaf is on the plant, its flavor can be either highly intense or very mild. The younger leaves at the top of the plant, having been exposed to the sun, offer the greatest richness of flavor, while the leaves at the bottom tend to be older, offering the least flavor. It's the way the cigar blends these different types of tobaccos together that makes it truly wonderful.

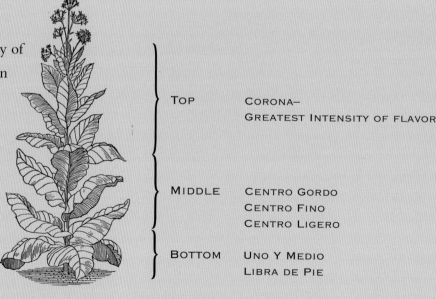

TOP   CORONA— GREATEST INTENSITY OF FLAVOR

MIDDLE   CENTRO GORDO CENTRO FINO CENTRO LIGERO

BOTTOM   UNO Y MEDIO LIBRA DE PIE

HECHO A MANO

Cuban cigars are the most sought-after prize in cigar smoking today, a veritable holy grail of the cigar sect. Due to a thirty-plus-year embargo on Cuban goods, Cuban cigars are about as available on U.S. streets as a cab in New York City when it's raining. But if you went to Cuba and thought you could get a decent Cuban cigar, think again.

One might imagine Cuba to be cigar smoker's paradise, where the world's best smokes are sold everywhere. However, tobacco is Cuba's fourth biggest export, behind sugar, nickel, and citrus fruit. This means that Cuban tobacco companies must apply all their resources to produce cigars for export, at the expense of the domestic market. While selecting and grading tobacco at the plantation, the top quality leaves are earmarked for export, leaving the sub par tobacco to be made into cigars for the domestic market. And recently, strict rationing has been necessary, as domestic cigar production has halved since 1990. The result? There are cigars available within Cuba, but they're not always the connoisseur's smoke you'd buy in a cigar shop in London.

This shortage of quality cigars within Cuba has led many a Cuban smoker to strive to become a cigar roller. A roller is an important and prestigious position in Cuba, requiring a long apprenticeship. But one of the most enjoyable benefits of the job is the fact that rollers can spend their work days smoking some of the world's best cigars!

Cigar makers at a cigar factory, Havana, Cuba.

CURING AND FERMENTING CIGARS

Once the leaves are picked they are brought to the curing barn, or *casas del tabaco,* where they are dried and air cured in a process that can take fifty days. Leaves are hung in pairs on poles, or *cujes,* to dry. Fifty pairs of leaves are hung on each pole, and hoisted high in the barn to ensure the right temperature and humidity. The leaves first turn yellow, then slowly develop the familiar brown color we all know. Over time, the poles are raised higher and higher in the barn. When finished, the leaves are lowered from their suspended state and move on to fermentation.

Leaves are then assembled into piles, first into small piles called *gavillas,* and then into larger piles over three feet high, called *pilónes.* Here, a slow fermentation process, similar to composting, reduces the resin in the leaves, yielding a more uniform color. The mois-

ture and the weight of the leaves in combination with the humidity of the barn causes the temperature of these piles to rise. If they get too hot, the piles are broken up, allowing the leaves to cool before being restacked. This fermentation process is one key distinction between cigar tobacco and cigarette tobacco. Fermentation mellows the tobacco and reduces tar and nicotine, producing a chemical change that leaves the tobacco with far fewer impurities.

At this point, the leaves then undergo a moistening, or *moja,* done with water or a combination of water and tobacco stems.

Left: Rene Martinez rolls one for his family's Don Rene line of cigars.

Right: Tobacco curing barn.

Fruits of the tobacco crop ready for sale, North Carolina, late nineteenth century.

The leaves are then stemmed and sorted, and sent to a storage place, or *escogida,* for months or in some cases even years. Finally, they are sent back to the fermentation area for a second round.

This second fermentation requires the leaves to be stacked in even bigger piles, called *burros,* which trigger a much more powerful fermentation effect. At this point the temperature will reach even greater heights, over 100 degrees in some cases. To monitor the temperature, large swordlike thermometers are plunged into the piles. One of the main impurities removed during this second fermentation is ammonia, and it is not unusual for the fermentation area to reek with the smell of ammonia as a result.

After this rigorous second fermentation, the leaves are left to rest on airing racks for a few days. They are then packed into bales, called *tercisos,* which are then wrapped in bark. The leaves can be stored in this state for various lengths of time. This aging process refines the flavor and aroma of the tobacco. This done, the leaves are now ready to be made into cigars.

HAV-A-TAMPA CIGAR CO., TAMPA, FLA.

110412

Cigar store Indian.
Late nineteenth-
century wooden
sculpture.

AU 10¢ Cigars

A CIGAR BY ANY OTHER NAME IS STILL A STOGIE

The "stogie" was a nickname given to a long cigar produced in the Conestoga Valley of Pennsylvania. By the end of the nineteenth century, the stogie was one of the most popular cigars in America.

The tercisos of leaves are shipped to the cigar factory, ready to be blended into any of a number of fine cigars. The leaves are stripped of their stems and sent to a grader who sorts them into piles according to size, color, and texture. At this stage, the leaves may be stored yet again for a period of up to two years.

The blending department, or *liga,* blends the different types of tobacco to make various types of cigars. Heavy security surrounds the blending process, for it is here that the trade secrets of the industry are kept. If you want to know what makes a Dunhill Corona a Dunhill Corona, this is the place.

Finally, after many months and many more pairs of intervening hands, the leaves are then sent off to the rollers, or *torcedores,* literally "twisters."

ROLLING CIGARS

Inside each cigar factory is the *galera,* the heart of the tobacco factory. It is here that the torcedores will apply their art to the tobacco leaves, transforming them into finished cigars. Each roller receives a daily allotment of tobacco from the blender. An experienced torcedore will produce over one hundred cigars in a single day.

A blend of filler leaves are gathered together and rolled into a binder leaf. No broken or shredded tobacco is used here, and

Left: The Cold War had Castro and Lenin keeping an eye on cigar rollers, 1964.

Right: A cigar roller's workshop. Colored wood cut, 1872.

excess is collected for use in cigarettes. This premature form is then pressed into wooden molds, the size of which are determined by the type of cigar being rolled. A wrapper leaf is then chosen and cut, by hand, to size. This is where the magic begins, for it is only with experience that the roller can utilize the perfect combination of finesse and accuracy to spin the fragile wrapper. Carefully the wrapper is stretched across the cigar, with a small piece of the wrapper used for the cap, or end of the cigar. Finally, the cigar is guillotined to the correct length, and the process is complete. A cigar is born!

THE READER: THE ROLLERS' RADIO

Rolling can be a slow job, and to break up the day, the rollers in Cuban factories appoint a lector, or reader, to keep them abreast of current news and literature. While the rollers, heads down, faithfully concentrate on producing fine cigars, the reader, chosen by the rollers, assumes a position at the front of the gallery, his words reverberating throughout the hall. The daily program will include news of the day, sports, and classic novels. Material to be read is chosen by popular vote, and has included fictional works as well as writings by Fidel Castro. At the end of the day, the reader is rewarded for his fine voice and paid by the rollers.

Cigar rollers are kept up-to-date by the reader, or lector.

The Anatomy Of A Cigar

Wrapper.

The wrapper is the most essential part of a cigar, as its character dictates the cigar's appearance. A wrapper leaf must be strong yet pliable enough to be stretched over the binder and the filler. Although quality wrappers come from Honduras, Costa Rica, and Mexico (and Cuba, of course), some of the most sought-after wrappers come from such exotic and unusual places as Sumatra and Connecticut!

Binder.

The binder is the crude, inside wrapper that holds the filler together. It is usually made from a tougher leaf, although quality is relevant. In Cuba, where the better tobacco is reserved for export, the same leaf used in a binder in a cigar earmarked for Europe could end up as the wrapper on a domestic cigar.

Filler.

The filler consists of a unique blend of whole leaves, running the length of the cigar. The combinations of which filler leaves are used, and how they are assembled, determines the cigar's overall character and taste. The leaves used in the filler are a combination of the more flavorful upper leaves of a tobacco plant and the lower leaves, which affect how the cigar smokes.

CHAPTER TWO

The Perfect prop: Cigars on Vintage Stage and Screen

*T*he cigar was omnipresent in the Hollywood of old. From the first cinematic hits of the thirties, right up to the sixties, some of the screen's biggest stars were regularly seen puffing on a stogie. This brings us back to an interesting and common debate about Hollywood. For all its glitz and glamour, does Hollywood reflect society, or influence it?

Does it pull, or does it push? While the armchair directors can debate the lofty theme of the cinematic effect on society for hours, it does bear mentioning that the cigar and the movies grew up together. The early male movie stars were more than cigar smokers—for many, it was an extension of their personality. For them, a cigar was much more than a cigar.

Left: W.C. Fields debates whether the pen is mightier than the cigar in *International House,* 1933.

CIGARS BEFORE CELLULOID

The bond between show business and cigars predates the dawn of cinema. Oscar Hammerstein I was undoubtedly one of the first links between the love of smoke and the

love of the stage. This early tobacco lover and opera entrepreneur was actually the grandfather of Oscar Hammerstein II, composer of such Broadway hits as *The Sound of Music, South Pacific, Oklahoma!,* and *Showboat.* It was his grandfather who gave the legendary tunesmith his first job in the theater business, and out of recognition for the elder Hammerstein's achievements the younger Oscar decided to append II to his name.

The elder Hammerstein had a long and rocky career in the theater, declaring bankruptcy three times in his life. But through it all, his tobacco business gave him the steady income necessary to navigate the stormy seas of show business. Oscar Hammerstein I held forty-two tobacco related patents, including the adjustable cigar case and the first cigar wrapping machine. In 1874, Hammerstein founded the *U.S. Tobacco Journal,* an important tobacco trade jour-

nal which is still published to this day. Ultimately, Hammerstein's love of the theater won out—he divested of the publication in 1888 to begin a long series of theater construction in what is now Times Square. But, Hammerstein remained a devout cigar lover, smoking twenty-five cigars a day.

More often than not, when we think about cigars and old Hollywood, it is the on-screen personalities that are cemented in our minds. The tradition started in old vaude-ville, where comics used the cigar as an integral part of their act. In the early 1900s, the cigar was a fixture in the mouths of most American males; it was said that two out of three men smoked cigars. But to the comedian on-stage, it was more than just a popular habit: The cigar was the important accessory that defined persona. A flip of the cigar in the mouth, arms folded, meant, "I'm standing my ground." A twirl of the stick in hand—accompanied by the raising of an eyebrow—was a clear "come hither" look to young women.

A cigar brought out the good, the bad, and the ugly in Clint Eastwood in *Christie,* 1972.

Charlie Chaplin's
Tramp enjoyed
one night of
cigar-filled glam-
our in *City Lights*,
1931.

GROUCHO LEAVES HIS MARK

If the use of cigars was a great comedic skill, Groucho Marx made it a high art. This master of facial expressions and stinging one-liners was never seen without his characteristic cigar, and early on he realized that the cigar was as integral to his character as his exaggerated mustache. But in the early part of his career, when Groucho was developing his cigar shtick with his comedic sidekicks Harpo and Chico, the cigar was responsible for a historic shift in their act that served as one of their legacies. It has been said that Harpo, the mute member of the team, began his lifelong silence when he was not given any lines in a particular production. But actually, it was a cigar that quieted him forever.

Of the hardworking Marx brothers, Groucho was the insomniac. The other boys, who slept late, left it to Groucho to arrive early at the theater and rehearse the orchestra. Early in their vaudeville career, legend has it that Groucho arrived for one of these rehearsals sporting, as always, a lit cigar. Rehearsal commenced, but soon an irate house manager stormed the stage, yanked

the flaming cigar out of Groucho's mouth and tossed it to the ground, pointing to a barely visible "No Smoking" sign. Adding financial injury to insult, the manager levied a five dollar fine on Groucho. A steamed Groucho continued with rehearsal, and told the other boys about the fine when they arrived for the evening's performance.

In another example of their perfect timing, the Marx Brothers waited till just before they were scheduled to go on stage, and proclaimed to the manager that they would not appear unless he rescinded the five dollar fine. The manager refused, and Chico declared the show canceled and started to remove his makeup. As the crowd grew impatient, Harpo stepped in with a compromise. If the manager would match their five dollars, and the ten dollar kitty could be handed over to the Salvation Army, the act would go on. With the roaring sounds of an unhappy crowd in his ears, the manager relented and the show was a smashing success.

Afterwards, the boys had less than an hour to undress and catch a train to their next performance. When they appeared in the manager's office, they found their pay waiting for them in four big canvas bags.

With a twirling cigar and a raised eyebrow, Groucho Marx, *left and right,* was a master of comic suggestion.

The manager was paying them in pennies! Enraged beyond belief, but desperate to catch their train, the boys counted one bag and decided the total was close enough. With no time to spare, the boys ran to their train, but not before Harpo would turn back to the manager and scream, "I hope your lousy theater burns down!" The next day, the Marx Brothers learned what power Harpo's words could have when they found out that the theater had in fact burned to the ground. It was decided right there that it was far too dangerous for Harpo to speak, thus sentencing him to a career of silence.

GROUCHO MARX ON CIGARS

As the king of cigar shtick, Groucho Marx and his ever-present stogie supplied an endless source of comedic material. His trademark wiggle of the eyebrows combined with a not-so-subtle shake of his cigar provided the one-two punch that made his one-liners so memorable. Here are a few of his smokiest . . .

How Groucho Started Smoking:

> *Groucho:* A cigar gave you time to think. You could tell a joke and if the audience didn't laugh you could take some puffs on the cigar . . .
>
> *Question:* And if the joke wasn't funny?
>
> *Groucho:* Then I'd use a different cigar.

The Scene That Got Cut:

> *Groucho:* So, Mrs. Smith, do you have any children?
>
> *Mrs. Smith:* Yes, thirteen.
>
> *Groucho:* Thirteen! Good lord, isn't that a burden?
>
> *Mrs. Smith:* Well, I love my husband.
>
> *Groucho:* Lady, I love my cigar but I take it out of my mouth once in a while.

Groucho, The Sports Fan:

> *Football Referee:* What are you doing with that cigar in your mouth?
>
> *Groucho:* Why, do you know a better way to smoke it?

"So I decided not to smoke. It was more fun to annoy the lady passengers."

—ERNIE KOVACS, WHEN TOLD HE COULD SMOKE
IF HE DIDN'T ANNOY THE LADY PASSENGERS.

THE CIGAR'S COMEDIC LEGACY

Marx was only one in a long line of cigar-chomping comedians. Ernie Kovacs, the insanely funny comedian who pioneered a kind of manic craziness that influenced David Letterman and Steve Martin, smoked over twenty cigars per day. Unfortunately, it was also his undoing. In early 1962, a well-liquored Kovacs was reaching for a cigar while driving, and subsequently wrapped his Corvair around a telephone pole. When the ambulance arrived, they found Kovacs had died, but not before he had managed to pull himself part way out the passenger door, his left hand reaching for the unlit cigar that had fallen on the ground.

Other comedians were members of the cigar lovers' club, too. The size of Jimmy Durante's nose correlated precisely to the size of his cigar habit. Jack Benny was also a fan, although one might wonder how much his notoriously tight budget allowed him to spend on smokes. Scowling and wrinkled, Walter Matthau brought an everyman's sensibility to his love of cigars as

Right: A cigar gave Jimmy Durante a good counterpoint to his major league schnazolla.

Jack Lemmon's grumpy roommate in *The Odd Couple*. "Mr. Television" Milton Berle was such a big cigar fan that he got his son into the act early on. Berle's son Bob Williams, now a manager of a Phoenix cigar shop, recalls how his father found him smoking a cigarette at age thirteen. Williams recalls that Berle "took a double Corona, stuck it in my mouth, and made me smoke. It was awful!" Later, Berle showed Williams the finer points, taking him to cigar dinners, and showing him how to pick and light them. Even the immortal W.C. Fields got into the cigar act. This great comedian, who once said, "Everything I do is either illegal, immoral, or fattening," made juggling cigar boxes part of his act, and a recurring gag had Fields confuse a candle with a cigar, smoking the candle and putting the cigar in the candle holder.

But of all the late, great funnymen known for cigar chomping, none was more identified with a long stogie than George Burns.
In a brilliant ninety-three-year career in

show business, Burns was seldom seen without his beloved El Productos. In his prime, Burns put away ten a day; by the time he reached one-hundred years old, the number had only gone down to eight. Burns' cigars are so closely associated with Burns' career and persona that the left imprint of his cigar is alongside those of

"Mr. Television"
Milton Berle
is one of
Hollywood's
great cigar lovers.

A grand Hollywood cigar entrance. *Left to right:* Gracie Allen, George Burns, Mary Livingston, and Jack Benny arrive for the premiere of *Hurricane* in 1937.

his hands and feet outside Mann's famous Chinese Theater in Hollywood. And in October of 1996, a Sotheby's auction netted $57,500 for his humidor. The humidor, given to Burns by the Cigar Institute of America, resembles a 1930s radio, and bears the inscription "Presented to George Burns, Cigar Smoker of the Year 1952."

WHERE THERE'S SMOKE, THERE'S BURNS

George Burns made a point of living the good life. During his one hundred years he enjoyed plenty of fine cigars, and produced a fine repertoire of one-liners on the joys of smoking.

"Happiness is: A good martini, a good meal, a good cigar and a good woman . . . or a bad woman depending on how much happiness you can stand."

"If I paid ten dollars for a cigar, first I'd make love to it, then I'd smoke it."

Never caught without his trademark El Productos, George Burns holds a press conference in London in 1982.

"I make movies to be able to smoke cigars for free.
That's why I write so many villains who chomp their cigars."
—ORSON WELLES

Orson Welles
relaxes with a
cigar on the set
of *La Ricotta* in
Italy, 1962.

THE GANGSTER'S UNIFORM: SUIT, TIE, HAT, CIGAR

In the Hollywood of old, cigar lovers came in all types, not just funny guys. For every stand-up that was punctuating a joke with a Macanudo, there were just as many cigar-chomping tough guys looking to "make it into the big time." For Hollywood gangsters, the cigar symbolized power and greed, and clearly emphasized their status as a "boss."

When considering the Hollywood tough guy and the cigar, one might again wonder if Hollywood reflects or influences society. For one of the most famous cigar-chomping hoodlums around, the answer was obvious. Edward G. Robinson ushered in a whole new generation of cigar bosses when he donned a stick in *Little Caesar.* So convincing was Robinson in the role of Rico Bandello, a small-time mobster who celebrated his making the big time with a ceremonial cigar, that a generation of screen gangsters followed his model. But if imitation is truly the sincerest form of flattery, the admiration of Bandello hit its zenith when real-life mob bosses began emulating Robinson's fictional gangster, donning the cigar as a sign of power.

While the comedian used the cigar to bring home a punch line or pause for effect, the gangster used the cigar as an article of intimidation, waving the butt at an adversary to punctuate a barrage of threatening rhetoric. It

OZARK CROOKS OZARK CROOKS OZARK CROOKS

Left: Edward G. Robinson uses a dangerous prop in *Key Largo,* 1948. The gun is quite intimidating, too.

Right: Paul Newman pulls a fast one in *The Sting,* 1973.

was a role that Robinson invented and mastered, and for a while he found himself typecast as the cigar-chomping hoodlum. But Robinson gradually broadened his range and proved to be a highly skilled actor. Often he'd drop the tough guy stance, but never the cigar. Even when playing a gentleman, as in the classic 1944 film noir, *The Woman in the Window,* the cigar was his companion.

Generations of cigar hoods followed Robinson's lead. Sheldon Leonard, the well-known character actor who made the black shirt and white tie the default gangster wardrobe, chomped his way through many a film. Orson Welles brought the cigar bit to its grungiest as a small-time law guy in *Touch of Evil;* Al Pacino joined the club as a Cuban mobster in *Scarface.* Even the animated Baby Herman got into the act, wisecracking his way through one-liners as a pint-sized roughneck in *Who Framed Roger Rabbit?*

Art reflecting life, or influencing it? Who knows? But one thing can be said for cigars and the movies—they've been inseparable from the beginning. And even now, as a whole new generation of stars discover the warm glow of a cigar, you can be sure that they'll carry that love with them offscreen as well as on.

Life influencing art? *Left:* Cigar chomping gun moll of the '30s, Bonnie Parker. *Below:* Faye Dunaway got all the details right, even the cigar, in *Bonnie and Clyde,* 1967.

Genuine and juvenile tough-guys. *Left:* Al Pacino in *Scarface*, 1983. *Right:* Baby Herman in *Who Framed Roger Rabbit?*, 1988.

Close, But No Cigar: A Sucker's Bet

During the late nineteenth and early twentieth centuries, traveling carnivals were among the most popular forms of entertainment in America. These roving bands of semi-legal swindlers were well known for their unique ability to extract goodly sums of cash from hardworking folk, only to pull up stakes and be gone the next day. One of their most profitable gimmicks played to a gentleman's ego, and as we all know, where egos go, cigars soon follow.

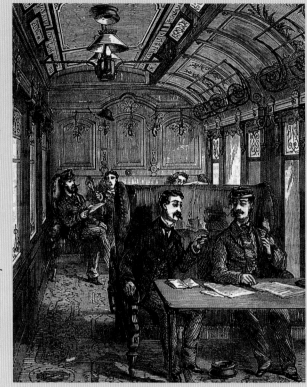

The sledgehammer game was a well-known test of strength at these carnivals. As a young man paraded by the booth with his date, the carnival barker would tease the sucker into impressing his lady friend by "ringing the bell and winning a prize." For a nickel, the contestant was given the opportunity to swing the sledgehammer onto a level, which sent a block sailing up a cable. If he swung hard enough, he'd ring the bell and win a cigar. Of course the barker really controlled the block, and would never allow the bell to ring on the first try. This failure was loudly announced by the barker's cry of, "Close, but no cigar!" Sweaty and humiliated, with a crowd gathering and his date watching anxiously, the young turk would pony up another nickel and try again. And again. And again. Soon the barker would have mercy and allow the exhausted and demoralized man to win and claim his cigar, but not before he'd spent the cost of an entire box.

Above: Lighting up on-board the Great Northern Railway. Etching, 1879.

Cigars were a common theme for vintage postcards in the early part of this century.

MARK TWAIN'S SMOKING ONE-LINERS

Mark Twain's taste in cigars, like his writings, were never high brow. It comes as no surprise that the man who made his fame writing about Huck Finn and Tom Sawyer paid four dollars a barrel for his cigars. Although his taste in cigars was pedestrian, Twain's cigar quotes were strictly top shelf.

Among some of his more memorable quips:

"To cease smoking is the easiest thing I ever did, I ought to know because I've done it a thousand times."

"As an example to others, and not that I care for moderation myself, it has always been my rule never to smoke when asleep and never to refrain when awake."

"To me, almost any cigar is good that nobody else will smoke, and to me almost all cigars are bad that other people consider good."

"If I cannot smoke cigars in heaven, I shall not go."

A connoisseur of bottom-shelf smokes, Mark Twain bought budget cigars by the barrel.

THE ASH: A LEGAL THRILLER

The cigar's usefulness as a prop goes far beyond the world of entertainment. All good trial lawyers know that success in the courtroom is ten percent facts, and ninety percent show-manship—the ability to sway a jury has much less to do with *what* you say than *how* you say it. Whether the goal is to gain a big settlement or a small prison sentence, a trial lawyer's main objective is to gain attention for his argument and distract the jury from the opponent's. Back in the early twentieth century, when the courtroom was a cigar-friendly environment, the notorious lawyer Clarence Darrow saw the value in this, and often used a cigar to sway a jury.

Darrow was rarely seen in the courtroom without a cigar. In fact, he was known to light up just as his opposition was to begin their case. As his opponents argued, Darrow's cigar ash grew longer and longer. Soon, the jury would take notice. Eventually, the jury was ignoring the case being presented, captivated by the gravity-defying ash poised precari-ously over Darrow's immaculate white vest. By the time he laid his smoke to rest, the courtroom knew more about Darrow's cigar than anything the opposition presented that hour.

What the jury didn't know was that the often-victorious Darrow prepared his own cigars ahead of time, com-plete with a straightened out paper clip rammed though the center. The paper clip ensured a long ash, and in many cases, a certain victory.

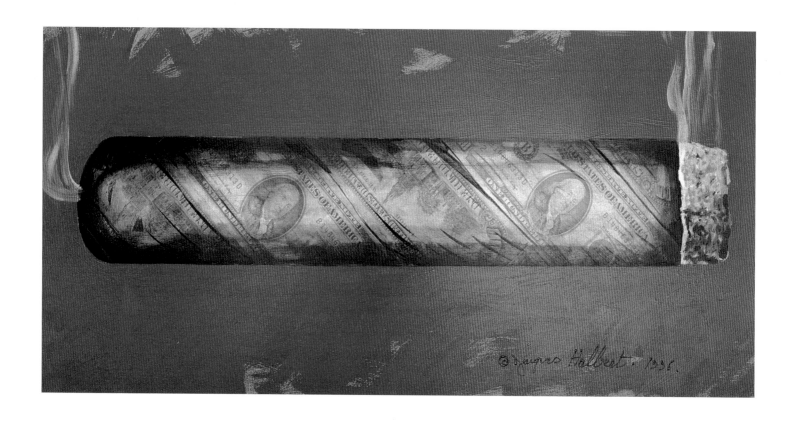

CHAPTER THREE

CIGARS IN SOCIETY

The world is a very different place than it was one-hundred, fifty, even twenty years ago. Over the years, world leaders come and go, technology evolves, clothing styles come into fashion, then go out, then come back again. But one thing has remained constant: a cigar smoker's love of the ritual. It's a love that only those who enjoy a fine smoke will appreciate. Whether it be the first Europeans on the shores of San Salvador enjoying a twisted stalk of dried tobacco leaves wrapped in corn husks, or a Manhattan socialite carefully lighting a forty-dollar Cuban amidst the posh surroundings of the Macanudo Club in New York City, the appreciation of the mellowing effects of a cigar transcend time.

Although this appreciation is omnipresent, the attitudes and opinions concerning cigar smoking have varied greatly over the years. In the last hundred years alone in the United States, we've seen cigar smoking go from a near-universal pastime, to a niche fancy of the older set, and back to the phenomenon it is today. Presidents of the United States have come full circle on the issue of cigars, from Warren G. Harding's campaign cigar bearing his portrait, to the "Just Say No" prudishness of Republicans from Eisenhower to Reagan,

Left: Burning Money, Jacques Halbert, 1996. Acrylic on canvas, 24 x 48 in. (70 x 122 cm).

and back again to Bill Clinton lighting up on the golf course. From Queen Victoria's tirades against tobacco to Freud's couch sessions with oral fixations, the cigar has done nothing if not generate passionate debate. If you're caught in the clutches of its alluring magic, a cigar has a special place in society; if you choose not to indulge, that special place is usually anywhere you are not.

This, unfortunately, has never changed. Today's cigar society concerns aficionados and foes alike. Its list of characters includes the royal and the regular, the famous and the forgotten, and the righteous and the repugnant.

A cigar fanatic, Winston Churchill once called Alfred Dunhill to check on his cigar stash after an air raid on London during World War II.

La Regenta, Dan
Douke, 1995.
Acrylic on three-
dimensional
canvas, 42 x 60 x
9 1/2 in. (107 x
152.5 x 24 cm).

THE MODERN RESURGENCE

Let's digress, if we may, to the topic of today's cigar culture. Notice we don't say trend or
fad—although today's explosive popularity of cigars could credibly be referred to by
either of these words. The current cigar boom has more to do with culture than the act
of smoking. Cigarmania has transcended the specifics of cigar brands and sizes; like count–
less other movements before it, cigars have permeated many parts of our life, and some
even say it has led to a revival of all things old and chic. It's larger than the cigar. Much
larger. But first, let's do the numbers.

A quick scan of a spreadsheet will attest to the fact that the cigar has burned its way
into American society. According to the Cigar Association of America, cigar sales increased
in 1994 for the first time since 1970. Sales in 1995 were nearly 2.6 billion cigars, and sales

Aspects of Suburban Life: Golf, Paul Cadmus,1936.

The Rabbis II,
Archie Rand,
1985. Acrylic on
canvas, 58 x 48
in. (147 x 122
cm).

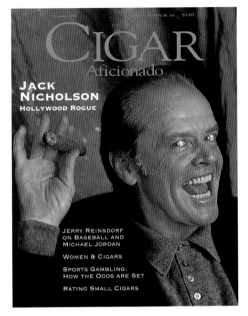

of premium cigars—the more expensive hand-rolled variety—rose over thirty percent. Although that's still a long way from the cigar peak of 1964, when nearly nine million cigars were sold, there's no denying the upward swing in this curve.

Much debate (and newspaper space) has been devoted to the question of why this resurgence has occurred, and why now. Although we can draw many conclusions from the changing habits of an aging baby boomer generation, most cigar

watchers put most of the credit (or the blame) squarely on the shoulders of one Marvin Shanken, publisher of *Cigar Aficionado* magazine. Legend has it that Shanken, who finished last in his class from the University of Miami, first got the whiff of a new trend while overseeing a glossy wine magazine called *The Wine Spectator*. In 1992, as the right-living, salad-chomping '80s came to a close, Shanken bucked the

trends and dared to introduce a glossy new ode to the high life. Its airbrushed pages offered more than cigar-related articles—they were a journal of the high and mighty, and ads for expensive watches and top shelf booze abound. Like any new movement, this cigar class needed a rallying point, and the swanky lifestyle depicted in the pages of *Cigar Aficionado* gave the new elite a flag to rally around.

Cigar-Friendly Restaurants and Lounges Around the World

Let's say you're planning a relaxing vacation—and relaxing, by definition, involves more than a few fine cigars. Or, perhaps you're simply planning an elegant dinner in your own home town, complete with an after-dinner drink and smoke. So, you figure you'll just pull a Romeo y Julieta out of your breast pocket after dinner and light up, letting the soft aroma of finely aged tobacco surround you as you take in the soft hum of other guests buzzing over their drinks and dinners.

Not so fast. One would think that in this era of cigar revival, finding a lively social atmosphere in which to enjoy a relaxing smoke would be as easy as finding a fellow smoker. But it is becoming increasingly difficult to find a cigar-friendly establishment in many major cities, as managers are forced—by simple economics and often local law—to banish smokers for the benefit of their non-smoking clientele.

A growing number of cigar-friendly lounges, bars, and restaurants still cater to smokers, but you'd better do your research before lighting up in public. A cyber-visit to CigarFriendly™ (http://www.cigarfriendly.com) beforehand will ensure that you find a classy, comfortable establishment that will welcome you and your stogie with open arms.

"Dedicated to providing the most comprehensive listing of cigar-friendly establishments and becoming the premiere cigar cybermall on the Web," CigarFriendly™ furnishes web-surfers with an international, up-to-date roster of restaurants and lounges hospitable to cigar smokers. From New York's famous Water Club to London's Savoy Grill, CigarFriendly™ searches the far corners of the planet to find places where you can kick back and smoke in peace.

Above: The posh digs of Shelly's Woodroast in Rockville, MD.

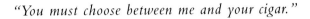

"You must choose between me and your cigar."
—BREACH OF PROMISE CASE, CIRCA 1885

THE LAST VICE

But can a single magazine have started all this? Some say it's a much deeper cultural phenomenon. Norman Sharp, president of the Cigar Association of America, claims that:

> "Cigars are so politically incorrect that it makes them more attractive to those who refuse to go along with the herd in today's militant neo-prohibitionist environment. We, as Americans, have two strong but diametrically opposed traits in our national character. One is the intense satisfaction of telling others what to do and how to live their lives. The other is an intense irritation at being told what to do and how to live our lives. Cigar smokers tend to be more independent and mature individuals who resent being told what to do, what to eat, what to drink. One observer claims cigars are the last vice left to men."

GOODBYE OLD FEL, I ISH GOIN TO GET MARRIED TOMORRER.

Strong words, but think about it. It's no coincidence that the resurgence of cigars comes off a period, the 1980s, where abstinence was the rule. Like a swing from a tree, the farther it goes one way, the wider the arch when it swings back.

"I was determined that I would smoke a cigar every day after luncheon and dinner."

—W. SOMMERSET MAUGHAM

Call it anything you want, populist fad or cultural revolution, but there's no denying that the cigar is at the center of a renewed consideration of the phrase "good for you." Abstinence has made way for moderation, and a whole new brand of young adventurers have used the "m" word as an invitation to live it up. Cigars are not the only decadence the nouveau swank have embraced. The venerable martini, long neglected as your parent's gin consumed during the Jurassic drunken business lunch, are now a mainstay at lounges that are popping up like olives in major cities. Beef is making a big comeback, as steakhouses such as Morton's of Chicago report booming sales at new locations around the country. And to show that nothing is sacred, sales of furs (a fashion statement so abhorrent in the eighties that donning one would surely get you kicked out of the best Los Angeles restaurant) were up in 1995 for the first time in years. To be fair, the lessons of the sober eighties are not totally behind us, as the war cry of "quality, not quantity" usually accompanies these lavish indulgences. These days, we might not spend the whole day socking back martinis and burning up stogies like they did in the fifties and sixties, but when we do indulge, it's top shelf all the way.

Left: The ultimate bachelor pad accessory. Hava Tampa Cigar advertisement, 1963.

Right: The End of a World, Hugo Cloud, 1989. Duraflex photograph, 14 x 11 in. (35.5 x 28 cm).

GRAND COUNCIL

TITLE & DESIGN OWNED BY H.W. & CO.

STRENGTH IN NUMBERS

Finally, no lifestyle shift would be complete without a forum to share it with others. Enter the "cigar dinner." Virtually unheard of a few years ago, the cigar dinner has become ground zero for the new cigar elite. Black tie revolutionaries have been bonding together since the first affair was held at the Boston Ritz Carlton in 1984, and in 1994 over 2,000 such events were held across America. The grand-daddy of these events, the *Cigar Aficionado* "Big Smoke," draws hundreds of people willing to pony up $150 to schmooze with like-minded renegades. Again we ask, trend or cultural revolution? Probably it's more of a bonding moment, as group smokes allow a large group of people to gather, indulge, and thumb their noses at society. If there's safety in numbers, these hoards are going to tackle the opposition in style.

The aristocracy lights up. *Left:* An antique cigar box label. *Right: The Opera Buff*, L. van de Gheynst, 1904.

CIGAR INTERNET SITES

The Internet has permeated all aspects of our life, so it should come as no surprise that cig-armania has hit cyberspace as well. When you think about it, it makes sense. The same group of people who have pushed cigars into the big time, young to middle-aged males with too much money and too much education, are also the ones surfing the net. Certainly both areas are becoming a little more fun now that women have dived in. Below is a list of notable cigar Internet sites. This is by no means an exhaustive list, but merely the cream of the crop.

Cigar Aficionado
http://www.cigaraficionado.com
The glossy print magazine takes it's blue-blood, over-the-top style to the Web. Lots of articles and info from the magazine and, of course, an online store to blow some cash in.

Cigar.com
http://www.cigar.com
A commercial site with a pretty extensive database of cigars that lets you search by brand, size, type and even country of origin. It also has tons of information on accessories, cigar stores, and cigar clubs.

CigarFriendly.com
http://www.cigarfriendly.com
A complete list of restaurants and lounges that will tolerate the big smoke. This snappy looking site includes cigar joints from Concord to Calgary, from Fresno to France.

The Cigar Internet Group
http://www.cigargroup.com
Arising out of the alt.smokers.cig-ars newsgroup, this massive informational site is the work of leagues of cigar toting volunteers under the direction of Bob Curtis, undoubtedly the foremost cigar guy on the Web.

The Cigar Journal
http://www.cigarjournal.com
This author's hilarious site of cigar stories. Every cigar is an adventure, and yours truly recounts his adventures smoking each one. Featuring the Five-Fidel Rating System.

Digital Havana
http://www.goldensection.com/havana
This site opens with "WARN-ING: A cigar with Jazz and a cold drink can seriously damage your productivity." Amen, brother.

FujiPub
http://www.fujipub.com
The foremost commercial cigar site on the Internet. Almost every cigar manufacturer of note has a presence here. There are tons of companies on the Web, but if they sell anything having to do with cigars, they're on FujiPub.

Holy Smoke
http://www.holy-smoke.com
A beautifully designed site created by one Father H, the largest cigar fan this side of, uh, heaven. The site includes the good padre's preferences in cigars, and a list of upcoming events.

Smoke Screen
http://www.smokescreen.com
Smoke Screen is a revolving door of cigar trivia. Each visit lists a different set of cigar facts, statistics and, well, useless information. But it's a lot of fun.

The Tobacconist
http://www.law.vill.edu/~kmortens/humidor
One cigar smoker's view of the Web, complete with a ton of links and a cigar chat, although not in real time. A good listing of commercial cigar shops on the Web, and a list of cigar reading material, from *The Cigar Journal* to Twain.

Whizstreet "Up in Smoke" Cigar Band Museum
http://www.mcs.net/~whizstrt/cigar.html
A cool non-commercial site dedicated solely to cigar band art. The images take a while to download, but they're worth the wait.

Cubist Potato
Cigar Holder,
Jacques Halbert,
1986. Mixed
media collage,
9¹/₂ x 14¹/₂ in.
(24 x 37 cm).

There's no denying that, as this new cigar fancy has soaked into our culture deeper than the sweet smell of cigars does into your clothing, it caught us off guard. Sharp points out that the industry "... never saw it coming. It took everyone by surprise." A little digging finds a 1992 article in *The Economist* that called Shanken's newly published magazine "a harder sell" than a wine magazine, and cites such foot-in-the-mouth observations as "few restaurants . . . tolerate even the faintest whiff of smoke from a stogie," and defines cigar smokers as "a niche market." But one thing's for sure: While attending a packed black-tie cigar dinner, sucking on a Robusto and ordering another martini, one cannot deny that a few years makes a world of difference.

BOYS AND THEIR TOYS:
THE HOLLYWOOD TRADITION CONTINUES

One thing is very obvious when you approach the front door of The Grand Havana

Room in Beverly Hills: There's no front door. For all the notoriety surrounding the country's most celebrated private cigar club, you'd think they'd hang out a shingle. But the gateway to this exclusive domain consists of nothing more than a single elevator, which will only rise to the correct floor with a special key. It's this key that brings you into the domain of Hollywood's cigar elite. This is where the big boys smoke.

Of course, cigars are no longer the exclusive territory of the male species. From George Sand's ground breaking puffs to Demi Moore's budget-breaking movies, cigars have now become a game anyone can play. But today, with the cigar culture reaching its apex, Hollywood's big boys are lighting up more than ever, and the list looks like a who's who of the big screen.

Not convinced? Well, let's return to The Grand Havana Room in Beverly Hills. Let's say you've begged, borrowed, or stolen the illusive key, and gotten past the friendly but watchful eye of the hostess (who, incidentally, knows every member by name). Since you've gotten this far, you slink through the glass door of the walk-in humidor. After looking over your shoulder, convinced you're not gonna get thrown out of the joint, you begin to examine the impressive wall of humidors in front of you. With lockers made out of the finest wood, the humidors run from the floor to the ceiling, over twenty feet above head. Amazed, you step a little closer and examine

The chic cigar clubs of America.
Upper left: Cuba Club, Miami, FL.
Above: The Grand Havana Room, Los Angeles, CA.

some of the names engraved in gold on the humidors. Arnold Schwarzenegger and Andy Garcia have humidors at convenient heights. Danny DeVito's is, predictably, one level lower. Mel Gibson. The Baldwin brothers. They're all here.

Look hard, and more often than not you'll see guys in the public eye donning a cigar. The well-known patrons of The Grand Havana Room have helped leap frog the hobby from personal habit, to private club, to the big screen, to your doorstep. And no one has worked harder at spreading the cheer of a good smoke than Arnold Schwarzenegger. The Terminator himself has been known to give away hundreds of cigars to his colleagues in Hollywood, and is said to have converted the likes of Carl Weathers and Danny DeVito. It may seem unlikely that a five-time Mr. Universe and seven-time Mr. Olympia became the ambassador of smoke, but let's just say he got some family assistance. Although he admits to lighting up once in a while in Germany as a body builder, Arnold inherited his true love of cigars from his father-in-law, Sargent Shriver, husband of Eunice Kennedy, sister to JFK—one of the many benefits of marrying into America's most celebrated family.

Arnold arrives, cigar in hand, at St. Francis Xavier Church for his wedding to Maria Shriver, of the Kennedy clan.

Danny DeVito, the
little guy with the
big appetite for
cigars.

David Letterman
follows in the
footsteps of such
cigar-chomping
wise guys as
Ernie Kovacs,
George Burns,
and Milton Berle.

"You ask me what we need to win the war? I answer tobacco as much as bullets."

—GENERAL JOHN J. PERSHING

You wouldn't expect Arnold to be a genteel smoker, and from looking at his arsenal of toys, you can tell he isn't. His lighters, the veritable torches that they are, have been described as "CIA assassin kits." The sight of Arnold on the streets of Los Angeles, smoking a cigar from behind the wheel of his Hummer (a massive military vehicle now available to civilians) is enough to dispel any notion of the gentleman smoker. But this is Hollywood, where true power doesn't come from physical strength, but from the power to yell, "Cut!" To this end, cigars have followed Arnold into the most powerful chair in town, as evidenced by his custom-made director's chair with an ashtray attached.

If you're looking to showbiz for a contrast to Arnold's massive cigar pecs, look no further than David Letterman. The antithesis of Schwarzenegger's tough stance, Letterman's love of cigars is pure New York smart aleck. His rise to the pinnacle of late night TV, and the advent of the '90s cigar craze, met head on during his 1992 announcement of his move to CBS. While staging one of the most anticipated announcements in television history, Letterman took in the spectacle from behind his Romeo y Julieta Churchill. Letterman's love of smoke had him chomping almost twenty cigars a day, until he abandoned the habit forever due to health concerns. But Dave always has the last word, and rumor has it that there's smoke seeping from his dressing room yet again.

"No woman should marry a man who does not smoke."
—ROBERT LOUIS STEVENSON

Tough guys and wise guys notwithstanding, many other Hollywood types can be seen haunting the deep velvet chairs of The Grand Havana Room on any evening. In waltzes Mel Gibson, a regular who likes to have dinner on the patio with a cigar before, um, another cigar. Gibson, winner of two Academy awards for *Braveheart*, was reportedly looking for a place to celebrate the night after the Oscar ceremony. His first choice? A smoke at The Grand Havana Room. Carrying his two "Golden Boys" with him to his private locker, Gibson found some spectacular congratulatory surprises: pre-Castro Romeo y Julietas! Gibson left that night with something to remember forever, and he took the Oscars along, too.

Look down the rows of humidors on the wall—way down—and again we see Danny DeVito. This world-renowned actor and director is also a big cigar fan. The diminutive, Emmy award-winning star of "Taxi," as well as many motion pictures, favors a good Cuban. He is such a fan, that in order to light up during one transatlantic flight, he personally asked everyone on the plane for their permission. So, who's gonna say no to Danny?

The list goes on and on. Bill Cosby has been a fan for life, having been exposed to cigars by his grandfather, who kept his cigars moist over a heating pipe in his basement.  Actor Jack Nicholson took up cigars as a way to quit smoking cigarettes, and claims to have learned the proper lighting of a cigar from Roman Polanski. Pierce Brosnan, Kurt Russell, Peter Weller—all well-known celebrities that enjoy a good smoke.

As the sun sets over Beverly Hills, bringing a soft, pink haze over The Grand Havana Room, we quietly lay down our cigars, now nothing more than smoldering stubs, and rise to leave. We look around, and silently say goodbye to all the fellow members, the stars, the agents and the ordinary blokes. "So long guys," you think, "See you tomorrow." Without turning, or even noticing your exit, they subconsciously bid you farewell, also looking forward to doing it again tomorrow.

Bill Cosby is a
modern-day
master at using
the cigar as a
comedian's prop.

FREUD: SOMETIMES A NEUROSIS IS ONLY A NEUROSIS

Sigmund Freud, quite possibly the world's first couch potato, had an answer for everything. From toilet training to dreams, it didn't matter what the subject was. If you had a problem, Freud could link it to sex and your mother. Seems his theories applied to everything and everybody, except himself. When confronted with the question that maybe he had fallen victim to one of his own neuroses theories, the imminently quotable Austrian physician did what he did best: He left us with a one-liner that sticks to this day. To explain his theory of oral fixation, Freud wrote the following:

"The fixation of the libido at pre-genital levels gives rise to adult neuroses, perversions, and strongly exaggerated forms of what we call normal behavior. If an infant passed through an entirely unsatisfactory oral stage or a traumatic one, much of his libido would remain fixated at this earliest stage of libidinal organization. A mother might frustrate the infant's intense desire to suck for pleasure and though no conscious memory of this traumatic event would remain, and given certain other developmental factors, this infant might well mature into an adult with an oral-fixation. His adult behavior would be in large measure the result of his infantile oral frustrations. His mouth would remain an overly cathected erogenous zone, and many of his adult behavioral patterns would manifest themselves as a search for oral pleasure. He might become a heavy smoker . . ."

An interesting argument, especially coming from someone who smoked incessantly. It seems Freud smoked over twenty cigars a day. You'd think someone who lit up as much as he did would be a little too close to the fire to comment on such things, especially since Freud was known to be extremely attached to his mother. But in the end, Freud ignored the advice of his doctors and continued smoking cigars. When asked how his lofty theories applied to him, his response was: "Sometimes a cigar is only a cigar."

Sigmund Freud never met a habit he didn't like to dissect, except his own cigar smoking.

WOMEN INVADE THE BOY'S CLUB

Many aspects of today's new cigar culture are very different than the cigar society of old. Not only are the cigars better and the prices higher, but the demographics have shifted. You don't have to have an MBA to notice that today's cigar

smoker is younger and hipper than the cigar chomper of old. Next time you cozy up to the bar at the Tosca Cafe in San Francisco, or sink into the velvet couches of The Grand Havana Room in Los Angeles, look around, and I'll bet you'll notice something else: Cigars are no longer the exclusive domain of men.

These days, women are making themselves right at home in the cigar world. Anne Archer is a perfect example. This Academy Award-nominated actress (*Fatal Attraction*) loves a good cigar, and isn't intimidated by the lack of female companionship. "I'm usually the only woman smoking," Archer told *Cigar Aficionado* magazine, describing her male-dominated cigar group, which includes her husband. "I'm very com-

fortable with cigars; I always have been." And why not? Cigars sure aren't the exclusive domain of old men the way they used to be. If a twenty-something male can savor cigar smoke between cheeks barely ready for a razor, women argue, so can they. In today's new cigar culture, every-

one is welcome. "It's a great social activity," says cigar fan/actress Demi Moore, "because there's something about smoking a cigar that feels like a celebration. It's like a fine wine."

A woman cigar smoker may seem unusual, but women and cigars have a long history together. Early travelers to the Americas report sightings of women and cigars. John Cockburn, an Englishman traveling in Costa Rica, reported in 1735, that "These gentleman gave us some seegars . . . these are leaves of tobacco rolled up in such a manner that they serve both for a

A female cigar roller puffs away at the Piedra Cigar Factory in Cuba.

German woman declare their independence at their afternoon smoking club in Berlin, Germany, 1937.

pipe and for tobacco itself. These the ladies, as well as the gentlemen, are very fond of smoking."

Although cigar smoking remained an almost exclusively male pleasure for centuries, there were notable exceptions. George Sand, a well-known gender-bender of the nineteenth century, was known to light up regularly. She earned a reputation for challenging the conventional role of the sexes, promoting ideas considered scandalous at the time. Sand frequently donned men's clothing, smoked daily, and had a romantic affair with Frederic Chopin. "The cigar numbs sorrow," Sand once said, "and fills the solitary hours with a million gracious images." Today, her spirit lives in the form of the George Sand Society, the mostly-female cigar smoking club that meets in New York and Los Angeles.

But, for the most part, women who smoked were rare in the past. Gertrude Stein was known to light up during her weekly salon, and Virginia Woolf would frequently join her husband for a cigar. French novelist Colette was said to be a fan, as was the poet and critic Amy Lowell. Even Annie Oakley was known to smoke a cheroot. But these women were the exception, rather than the rule. The notorious separation of women and cigars came to head in 1886, when Rudyard Kipling, foot firmly in mouth, wrote that "A woman is only a woman, but a good cigar is a smoke."

With provocative writing and a taste for cigars, George Sand challenged the traditional role of women in society.

Left: A bad cigar or a lover gone AWOL? Something rubbed Lucille Ball the wrong way in *Lover Come Back,* 1946.

QUEEN SEAL
MILD QUALITY CIGAR

The twentieth century brought a trickle of cigar women, and the maverick actress Marlene Dietrich was one of the first. Dietrich loved to shock people by lighting up, and smoked her way through a legendary cameo opposite Orson Welles in *Touch of Evil*. Fifties television icon Lucille Ball was known to enjoy cigarillos. By the time Julie Andrews donned a tux and cigar in *Victor/Victoria*, the male-only cigar walls were starting to crumble.

In 1994, the walls came down altogether, starting with an appearance by Madonna on *Late Show with David Letterman*. Even Letterman, himself a high profile cigar smoker, was taken aback by Madonna's flaunting of a stogie. But by then, it hardly mattered. The flood gates opened, and a whole new generation of women had publicly declared their love of cigars.

Vanessa Williams brings grace, beauty, and a cigar to the opening of *Eraser* at Mann's Chinese Theatre, Hollywood, 1996.

What is it that attracts women to cigars? The same thing that brings men the pleasure of a fine cigar: the experience. "It's like an agreement you make with yourself," said actress/model Lauren Hutton in an interview with *Cigar Aficionado* magazine, "to take the time to relax and smoke a cigar."

Today, the list looks like a who's who of celebrity women. Whoopi Goldberg, supermodel Linda Evangelista, and actress Tia Carrere are avid cigar smokers. Turn on the tube any night, and you might see Julia Louis-Dreyfus chomp a cigar on *Seinfeld*, or catch former Ivory Soap baby Brooke Shields saddle up to the bar, cigar

in hand, on *Suddenly Susan*. Diane Keaton, Bette Midler, and Goldie Hawn are seen waving stogies in the poster for the movie *First Wives Club*.

By the time superstar Demi Moore appeared on the cover of *Cigar Aficionado* magazine, the arrival of the woman cigar smoker was complete. "I like the flavor," Moore said in the article, "I like the taste. I enjoy the smell of a good cigar. It relaxes me."

Men, get used to it. Just as women have broken down other walls in our male-dominated society, the walls of the men's-only cigar world, like the ash of a smoldering Cohiba, are falling too.

Hollywood women discover cigars in a big way. *Above:* Demi Moore graced the cover of *Cigar Aficionado* magazine. *Right:* Bette Midler, Goldie Hawn, and Diane Keaton burn fat ones in a promo for *The First Wives Club*, 1996.

CHAPTER FOUR

STORING, CUTTING, AND LIGHTING

*S*ome say a cigar is like a fine wine or cheese: It must be chosen carefully, stored carefully, and served at just the right time. Others say, "What the hell, a smoke is a smoke and

anyway, you're gonna put a match to the damn thing so what does it matter where you store it and how it gets lit."

As things go, the truth lies somewhere in the middle. For every Bronx Bomber who keeps their cardboard box of El Productos in the refrigerator, there's a sleek Los Angeles yuppie who goes overboard with $1,000 humidors and $200 cutters. The trick is knowing what is essential to the smoking experience, and what is high-priced fluff. Sometimes, it's not so easy to tell.

Right: Cigars and accessories by Davidoff.

Size Doesn't Matter . . . Or Does It?

When choosing from the thousands of varieties of cigars available, it's easy to get confused about what shape and size to buy. Is a small cigar better? Does a large cigar smoke cooler? The answer to both is: It depends. While size and shape alone tell you very little about the cigar, most smokers do have a personal preference for certain types. Although smokers will tell you that a larger cigar smokes cooler because the smoke has farther to travel, and a smaller cigar is less wieldy and easier to manage and keep lit, it's up to the individual smoker to decide what's best for them. To help in this effort, here's a general guide to the sizes and shapes of cigars.

Cigars are measured in two ways: length and girth. Length is measured end to end, in inches; girth is measured on a scale called "ring gauge." One ring is one sixty-fourth of an inch, making a 64-ring gauge cigar an inch in diameter. Below is a visual guide of the more popular sizes.

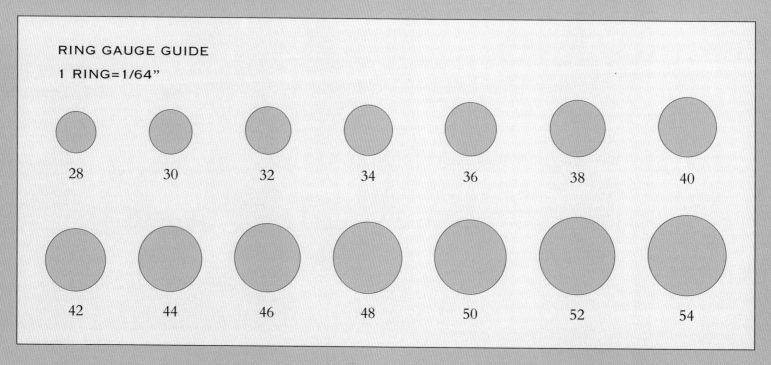

RING GAUGE GUIDE

1 RING=1/64"

28   30   32   34   36   38   40

42   44   46   48   50   52   54

"A special type of cigar was produced by the Marsh factory in Wheeling, West Virginia. It was particularly popular with the teamsters who drove the great lumbering Conestoga wagons along the National Road. It was corruption of this word, Conestoga, that led to the creation of the term "stogie" to describe any cigar."

—DICTIONARY OF AMERICAN FOLKLORE

CHOOSING A CIGAR

Take, for example, the exercise of choosing a cigar. Walk into one of the country's premier cigar stores and you'll be inundated with countless sizes, shapes, and varieties. Now, I'm not going to tell you what to buy, but here are some tips on how to tell if you're buying a fresh bunch or yesterday's bananas.

Let's say you've just walked into your local tobacconist, and you're ready to plunk down some serious cash for a premium cigar. Here's what to look for. First, do a visual inspection. Even to an untrained eye, a cigar should look "good": That is to say, the wrapper should be smooth and slightly oily. If the wrapper looks like it is beginning to unravel at all, it hasn't been properly cared for. See if there is any obvious discoloration in the cigar, and make sure the cigar isn't lumpy in spots. If you're buying a box, make sure the color is consistent across the entire box— any tobacconist worth his stuff will allow you to open the box and inspect the cigars. Finally, check the veins in the tobacco: They can be visible, but not unsightly or large. A good rule of thumb is that if it looks bad, it probably is.

Next, smell the cigar. Don't worry, you don't have to be Marvin Shanken to know what a cigar should smell like. It should smell, well, good. No pungent odors or musty smell. Smell the cut end, and even smell the box that the cigar came from.

Above left: The cream of Fuente's crop, the Opus X line of cigars.

Left: Leslie Caron demonstrates how not to test a cigar in *Gigi*, 1958.

Above right: Cigar store Indian woman, by C.J. Hamilton. Colored drawing, 1840.

Now, feel the cigars. The old adage is to hold the cigar up to your ear and roll it between your fingers—by doing this, you might be able to tell from a crunching sound that the cigar is dried out, but you may also end up damaging the cigar. The best thing to do is just gently press the cigar between your fingers. It should give a little. If it doesn't, it may be packed a little too tightly and may be tough to smoke. If you hear it crack a little, put it back and on the way out tell the tobacconist to turn up his humidor.

I wish I had a nickel for every time someone asked me whether the aluminum tubes or the cellophane hurt or help a cigar's freshness. The answer is no and no. For all the dubious claims, very few aluminum tubes are a substitute for a good humidification system. Conversely, if you put the cigar in the humidor in the tube, that won't hurt either. Most tubes have a little air leak anyway, so the air will get into the tube. This is good in the humidor, but bad as a storage device. If someone tells you the tube is a substitute for a good humidor, don't believe them. Same goes for cellophane. It doesn't hurt to keep the cigar in the cellophane, as long as it's in a good humidor.

WHAT'S IN A NAME?

By tradition, certain cigar shapes and sizes are given names. For example, a short, fat cigar is commonly referred to as a Robusto, and a skinny, long cigar is often called a Panatela. However, time has not been particularly kind to the cigar name, and today we find the names more of a guide than a strict rule. Why? Because cigar sizes are not standardized. Hence, one company's Corona may be a half of an inch longer and one ring gauge bigger than another. But names are still a good general indicator of size and shape.

NAME	LENGTH	RING GAUGE
Panatela	5–7 in. (12.5–17.5 cm)	30–34
Rothchild/Robusto	4.5–6 in. (11.25–15 cm)	48–50
Lonsdale	6.5–7 in. (16.25–17.5 cm)	40–43
Corona	5–5.5 in. (12.5–13.75 cm)	40–43
Churchill	7–7.5 in. (17.5–18.75 cm)	48–50

CUTTING YOUR CIGAR

OK, so you've made your purchase and rushed home to have a good smoke. Now comes time for the most ceremonial, but tricky part of the game—cutting the cigar. In the old days, it would suffice to just chomp the ends off and light up. But when you're in the world of premium cigars, somehow it doesn't seem right to take a bite out of a ten-dollar Avo Uvezian. A surgeon's cut is required.

There are basically three kinds of cigar cuts. The first is a "V" cut, where a wedge the shape of a "V" is sliced out of the top of the cigar from side to side. Once a very popular cut, the "V" has lost favor among today's aficionado for many reasons. First, it gives a very asymmetrical feel to the cigar. As you smoke it, you're bound to find a position for the cut relative to your mouth that you like. This could make the cigar burn unevenly. Second, with a "V" cut there's a very good chance, if you're one of those sloppy smokers who drenches your smoke in spit, that the "V" could collapse on itself. The cut leaves no support around the ends. Also, the "V" cut is a bear to get right, and at the prices of premium cigars, you don't want to leave much trial and error to the cutting process. Finally, "V" cutters are hard to come by, and when you do find them, they'll set you back plenty.

The second kind of a cut is a "punch" (or "pierce") cut. This is where you simply punch a hole in the end of the cigar. Advocates of a punch cut say that you're less likely to rip the end cap of the cigar, and by cutting as little as possible you're leaving a good majority of the end of the cigar intact. This can be accomplished a couple of ways. The more barbaric method is to thrust a wooden match down the end of the cigar. This method does nothing more than tear the wrapper,

Cutters a surgeon would be proud of from Bulgari, *upper right,* and Solingen, *far right.*

Left: Where the stars store their cigars: The humidor at The Grand Havana Room, Los Angeles, CA.

Toulouse-Lautrec,
M. Louis Pascal,
1893.

crunching the end leaves in the process. More expensive pokers are basically the high-end equivalent of the match thrust. A better way to achieve this cut is through a "bullet" cutter that bores out the end of the cigar. Much like an apple corer, this cutter is a

small circle of sharp metal that gets thrust into the end and delicately removes a core of tobacco. Some bullet cutters even have a little button that thrusts the metal deeper into the cigar. It's similar to a machine that takes soil samples, if you've ever seen one of those. I must admit that, for a long time, this was my preferred way of cutting a cigar. I liked how it left the basic shape of the cigar intact. But in the end, I found that this manner of cutting sometimes left a cigar difficult to draw, something that I (and most smokers) really hate. In the end, I found a guillotine cut to be the best.

A guillotine cut is, just as the name implies, a small blade that makes a horizontal slice off the end of the cigar. Everywhere I go these days, there seems to be the unanimous conclusion that the guillotine cut is the way to cut a cigar. And for good reason: A guillotine cut leaves a nice smooth edge, a symmetrical smoke, and plenty of opening for smoke to come through. Guillotine cutters are also cheap and easy to come by. But make sure the blade is sharp—there's nothing worse than the look and feel of a ragged end of a cigar after it's met a dull guillotine blade. The trick to this cut is chopping off just enough of the end of the cigar. How much is enough? Look at a cigar end, and you'll see where the cap meets the wrapper. Cut just above this line, leaving just a little cap left to hold the wrapper on.

LIGHTING

Here we go again, another controversy. You'd think that putting a match to a cigar would be easy, but not so. Aficionados will tell you that you can't just thrust a match into the end of a cigar, you have to toast it in a particular way. Although I will agree that fine tobacco will taste somewhat different depending how you light it, let me spell out for you the textbook way to light a cigar, and you decide. First, always use a wooden match or butane lighter. A wooden match because it has fewer chemicals in it, butane because it's odorless. For this example, I'll assume we're using a match. Light the match and let the flame die down, allowing the sulfur smell to dissipate. Slowly heat the end of the cigar with the match, rotating to get it all around. Why? This method helps you to get the entire cigar lit. Especially when you're smoking a big cigar, it's easy to get just one side lit, causing a lopsided smoke.

Be sure not to let the flame touch the end of the cigar. Once the entire end is sufficiently roasted, take an easy puff and let the flame come to the cigar. Again, don't let the flame hit the cigar. Puff slow, and rotate the cigar so you get the entire end lit. However you light it, once the thing is blazing, take your time. Smoke slow, and relax. You're not only doing yourself an injustice by hurrying your way through a smoke, you might also ruin a good cigar. A cigar smoked too quickly can get too hot and taste harsh.

But what about the band? Another popular question is whether or not to remove the band. Many highfalutin smokers tell you to keep the band on,

Left and above:
Colibri's
Churchill V
combination cigar
cutter/lighter.

unless you're ashamed of what you're smoking, as it's a sign of good taste. These are also probably the same folks who take the Armani tag out of their suit and sew it on the outside. In the beginning, the cigar band was created to protect royal fingers from stains of a cigar. Today, they're mainly for show and brand recognition. There is actually one good reason to keep a band on. As they are often glued on, removing them can sometimes rip the wrapper leaf. If you do remove them, wait until your cigar has warmed up a little, then gently tear off the band. For me, I always remove the band, if for no other reason than to stimulate conversation. Unless you do, how else can someone come up to you and ask, "So, whatta ya smokin'?"

Cigar Namesakes

In My Dreams: "I'll Take A Box Of Red Howards"

Only a select few have had the honor of having a cigar size named after them. This exclusive club of cigar namesakes includes some of most well-known cigar lovers of the past.

Churchill

If sheer volume is what it takes to get a cigar shape named after you, Sir Winston Churchill must be the model. This famous English statesman, who called cig-

ars "an absolute sacred right," smoked almost ten cigars a day. Unlike the man himself, a Churchill cigar is typically a tall cigar, ranging from seven to eight inches (eighteen to twenty centimeters) in length. So well known was his love of cigars that, after one particular Nazi bombing of London, Alfred Dunhill himself called Churchill to assure him his private stock of cigars was safe.

Lonsdale

It was in the early part of this century that the Earl of Lonsdale had a special cigar shape made just for him. The Rafael Gonzales Lonsdale, complete with a picture of the Earl, was soon the most exclusive cigar to come out of Cuba. Today, the Lonsdale is typically a longer, thinner cigar.

Rothschild

In the late nineteenth century, an impatient London banker named Leopold de Rothschild commissioned a Hoyo de Monterrey to make a shorter cigar that wouldn't take a long time to smoke. Hence, the Rothschild was born. Under five inches (thirteen centimeters) long, the Rothschild is one of the shortest cigars made. This classic cigar size is still available, but many times it's called a Robusto.

Left: One of the great men of smoke, Winston Churchill.

STORING

Keeping cigars in top shape is not rocket science. All you have to keep track of are two things, humidity and temperature. Cigars are creatures of habit, and long to be kept in a climate similar to the one they were born in. And as you might (or might not) remember from your last margarita-laden Caribbean vacation, that means warm temperature and relatively high humidity. Good cigar storage does require you to remember some numbers: 70-70. Seventy percent humidity, and seventy degrees. This is the optimal environment for a cigar. And of these two numbers, humidity is the most important. If a cigar gets too dry, it'll dry out and crack. Too moist, and it'll break out in green fungus, and maybe even get bugs. How attractive.

In theory, it doesn't matter how you achieve this climate for your cigars. Some people keep their cigars in a plastic bag with a sponge in it. Some use Tupperware, others a mason jar. But most use the time-honored humidor. The best humidors are made of cedar, for two reasons. First, cedar is good at retaining and releasing moisture to help ride out humidity swings. Second, it is also good for aging cigars because it gives a little spicy flavor to the smoke.

As important as what you keep cigars in are devices that keep track of the climate. A hygrometer is a nifty little gauge that measures humidity. It can either be an old-time brass analog dial, or a new fangled LCD readout. But what-

Right:
Humidor by
David W. Dyson.

ever the style, a hygrometer is an indispensable item. There are also small, inexpensive hygrometers on the market that will also record the temperature. A great tool because remember, it all boils down to temperature and humidity.

Humidors have always been more than a simple storage devices, and over the years they have developed into serious pieces of furniture. Today, the choice of humidors is staggering, and one can spend anywhere from a couple hundred bucks to thousands on a humidor. Cedar is preferred, but there are plenty of fine humidors made of other quality (and more exotic) woods. The main things to look for are that the box is air tight, and that it's the right size. My first humidor was a small one, and when someone sent me a bunch of Churchills, they had to sit sideways on top of my Panatelas. Also, it's foolish to buy a 150-cigar humidor if you're not an avid smoker, unless you're looking to age cigars. In today's cigar–crazed marketplace, some manufacturers are known to sell a cigar or two before their time.

A Davidoff dream case of cigars and cognac.

Artist unknown.
Cigar box pin
cushion, circa
1880-1920.

Many of these green smokes need more time, and cigar fans—burned by today's shortages—have been known to hoard boxes of their favorite brand. Consider it the wine cellar of smokes.

Last thought: Got a brother-in-law who insists that the best place to store cigars is the refrigerator? Don't listen to him. The refrigerator might be great for cantaloupe, but it's murder on cigars. Most refrigerators are dry as dust, and will dry out a cigar in no time. Plus, who knows what funky flavors the cigar will pick up while in a refrigerator. Trust me, an onion-flavored Macanudo ain't that great.

Cigar jewelry for the truly obsessed. *Left to right:* Mayor's gold and diamond cigar cufflinks and tie tack, and Hoyo de Monterrey cufflinks.

"I'M SORRY, YOU WANT *HOW MUCH* FOR THAT HUMIDOR?"

Next time you stroll into a Dunhill store and nearly faint at the price of a good humidor, take heart. You could have paid more. Much more. As did Marvin Shanken, publisher of *Cigar Aficionado* magazine. At a 1996 Sotheby's auction for the estate of Jacqueline Kennedy Onassis, Mr. Shanken had his eye on a historic humidor owned by JFK. Maybe he should have kept his other eye on his wallet. Before he was done, Shanken walked away with the box, to the tune of $574, 500.

The big loser in the process was Milton Berle. The famous TV comedian, and cigar lover, gave President Kennedy the humidor as an Inaugural Day present in 1961, and was hoping to buy it back and donate it to the JFK library. "To JFK," read the engraving on the humidor, "Good Luck, Good Health, Good Smoking, Love Milton Berle, January 20, 1961." But in the end, money won out over sentiment. Berle dropped out at $200,000, and Shanken kept bidding right past half a million bucks. A disappointed Uncle Milty went home empty-handed.

Right: No doubt about it, Jackie (shown with second husband Aristotle Onassis in 1974) had a thing for cigar smokers.

CHAPTER FIVE

A CATALOG OF FINE CIGARS

"What this country needs is a really good five-cent cigar."

—THOMAS RILEY MARSHALL, WHILE
PRESIDING OVER THE SENATE

Go to your local cigar shop. Attend a cigar dinner. Pick up a copy of *Cigar Aficionado* or *Smoke* magazine. What's the first thing you notice? A dizzying array of cigar brands. One of the most difficult choices facing a new cigar smoker is choosing from the enormous number of cigar brands on the market. Many, like Fuente and Macanudo, are well-known brands that require little introduction. Unfortunately, it's this notoriety that has caused better known cigars to be in short supply. But that's not to say that a lesser known brand isn't up to snuff. Quite the contrary. Don't be turned off by a brand you don't know. At the same time, don't assume just because a cigar has a fancy name you're going to like it. Remember, you're smoking the cigar, not the name.

Here is a short list of quality cigar manufacturers, their country of origin, and a little blurb about them. The list is hardly exhaustive, but a good place to start when shopping for cigars.

"The need for seductive labels has vanished. Men who buy
their cigars by name and number are blind to the banishments
of heroic Seglindes prone on the inside of a Cuban box."

—*FORTUNE* MAGAZINE, 1933

ARTURO FUENTE - DOMINICAN REPUBLIC

The Fuente family heritage is well known in the cigar world, and today members of the family still run the Fuente factory, and appear in their advertisements. The Fuente line of cigars is known for a mild quality and outstanding workmanship.

ASHTON - DOMINICAN REPUBLIC

Made at the Fuente plant, Ashtons are named after a well-known English pipe maker. Debuting in 1985, Ashton is best known for their Cabinet Selection cigars, an aged cigar popular in the United States.

AVO UVEZIAN - DOMINICAN REPUBLIC

When Avo Uvezian, composer of "Strangers in the Night," intro–duced his line of cigars in 1986, he immediately had another hit on his hands. The Avo has quickly gained a reputation as one of the finest cigars on the market. Premium construction and rich flavor make their hefty price a bargain.

BOLÍVAR - CUBA

Sporting a fancy label donning Simón Bolívar, who led Venezuela in a nineteenth-century revolt against Spain, the Cuban Bolívar is a powerful smoke. The trick is knowing which one to smoke. The brand sports almost twenty varieties, so find the one you like before you pony up for a box.

COHIBA - CUBA

Cohiba started production in the mid-sixties as the exclusive cigar for Fidel Castro and other Cuban dignitaries. After years of legendary unavailability, the illusive Cohiba (the Taino Indian word for "tobacco") was made available to Europe. Today, its bold flavor is one of the most sought-after in the world.

DAVIDOFF - DOMINICAN REPUBLIC

Besides swanky stores featuring everything from ties to luggage, Davidoff has been known to put out a good cigar or two. One of the few "outsiders" allowed to create a Cuban brand, Davidoff's produced a popular Cuban cigar until a much celebrated break with the Cuban state-run tobacco ministry in 1990. Since then, the fine taste of Davidoff cigars have come from the Dominican Republic.

DON DIEGO - DOMINICAN REPUBLIC

These fine cigars were the creation of one of the first cigar makers to leave Cuba after the revolution. Made in the Canary Islands until the 1970s, today's Dominican-made Don Diegos are made from Connecticut and Cameroon wrappers.

DON LINO - HONDURAS

A newer name on the scene, Don Lino has been making excellent Connecticut-wrapped cigars since 1989.

DON TOMÁS - HONDURAS

The Don Tomás brand has been around for over twenty years, and the company's wide distribution has made this medium-bodied cigar, even with today's cigar shortages, one of the most available on the market.

DUNHILL - DOMINICAN REPUBLIC

This beloved English name originally donned a line of Cubans in the 1980s, but soon after reverted to Dominican-made cigars. The company's distinctive blue and white label is always an assurance of the finest quality smokes.

FONSECA - DOMINICAN REPUBLIC AND CUBA

Originally a Cuban brand, this well-known name is now made in the DR, but a limited variety of Cuban-made Fonsecas still exist. Pick wisely from their quality, yet spotty, selections.

GRIFFIN'S - DOMINICAN REPUBLIC

Griffin's were a secret in Geneva until they were discovered by Zino Davidoff, and today they're known as quality, and pricey, cigars.

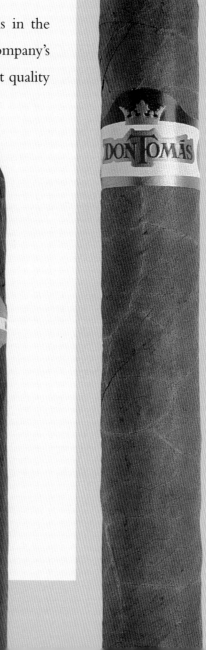

H. UPMANN - DOMINICAN REPUBLIC AND CUBA

Upmann's are one of the most widely distributed cigars on the market, and are known for their trademark metal tube. Although they're not high art, Upmanns are still a good beginner cigar.

HENRY CLAY - DOMINICAN REPUBLIC

More people know the name Henry Clay as a cigar brand than a politician, but it's the eighteenth-century senator that is the namesake of this working person's, full-bodied cigar.

HOYO DE MONTERREY - HONDURAS AND CUBA

Originally a Cuban brand, this venerable brand is still produced there, but it pales in comparison to the extraordinary Hoyo made in Honduras. Mild and smooth, the Honduran Hoyo de Monterrey and the Hoyo de Monterrey Excalibur are in a league of their own.

JOYA DE NICARAGUA - NICARAGUA

Like its country of origin, the Joya de Nicaragua brand (and its quality) has experienced much turbulence over the past twenty years, but recent offerings show hope that this "jewel of Nicaragua" will soon regain its once-spotless reputation.

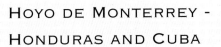

JUAN CLEMENTE - DOMINICAN REPUBLIC

No one debates whether to take the band off this Dominican cigar before smoking it. You have to, since it's wrapped around the cut end of the cigar. This fine brand is long on taste, yet short on supply, due to its tiny plant.

LA GLORIA CUBANA - UNITED STATES AND CUBA

A well-known Cuban brand, it is the American La Gloria Cubana that has been getting a lot of attention. Lovingly produced in Florida by Ernesto Carillo, this full-bodied cigar emulates a classic Cuban smoke in every detail.

LA PLATA - HONDURAS

Operating out of Los Angeles, La Plata has come to be known as one of the best kept secrets in America. Since 1947, Victor Migenes and family have created a truly fine smoke worthy of wider attention. It's just a matter of time before the world discovers the fine, mellow, sweet flavor of a La Plata.

MACANUDO - JAMAICA AND DOMINICAN REPUBLIC

Originally made in Jamaica, and now also in the DR, the Macanudo's consistent quality makes it tough to tell what country it comes from. Whatever the origin, Macanudo is a household name of cigars in America, and is a great bread and butter smoke.

MONTECRISTO - CUBA

More Montecristos come out of Cuba every year than any other cigar. Not to be confused with the Dominican variety available in the United States, the Cuban Montecristo typifies the full-bodied taste that has come to stereotype (for better or worse) a Cuban cigar.

MONTECRUZ - DOMINICAN REPUBLIC

If the Montecruz label looks suspiciously like that of the famous Montecristo, it's no accident. The family that owned Montecristo started this brand in 1964 for Dunhill, and today continues a tradition of fine cigars available in a dizzying array of sizes.

NAT SHERMAN - DOMINICAN REPUBLIC

The legendary New York cigar store of the same name launched their own line of cigars in 1993. With Big Apple inspired names like Gotham and City Desk, the tasty Nat Sherman (or "Shoyman" as the natives say) has been a favorite son ever since.

PARTAGAS - DOMINICAN REPUBLIC AND CUBA

One of the oldest cigar brands in Cuba, cigars with the Partagas brand now also come out of the DR. The Cuban stalwart is famously rough and abrasive, while its expensive Dominican cousin is known to have less rough edges.

PAUL GARMIRIAN - DOMINICAN REPUBLIC

You wouldn't think that a rich, DC banker could make a good cigar, but when Paul Garmirian launched his namesake in 1991, it proved to be everything a fine cigar should be. When you can find them (and afford them), P.G.'s are packed full of flavor, well-constructed, and a delight to smoke.

PLEIADES - DOMINICAN REPUBLIC

A French brand, Pleiades is as well known for its box (with built in humidifier) as it is for its cigars. Nevertheless, its mild taste has made it a favorite.

PUNCH - DOMINICAN REPUBLIC AND CUBA

Another old Cuban name, you will now find the brand coming out of the DR as well. The Dominican Punch is a wonderful, smooth smoke, while the typically full-bodied Cuban packs a, well, you know.

ROMEO Y JULIETA - DOMINICAN REPUBLIC AND CUBA

Another Cuban brand that is also made in the Dominican Republic, Romeo y Julieta is one of the best known Cuban names. The Cuban model is full-bodied, while the Dominican is more subtle.

TEMPLE HALL - JAMAICA

An old Cuban brand name, the Temple Hall has just recently been reintroduced. It is slowly acquiring a reputation as a fine, mellow smoke.

ZINO - HONDURAS

A Honduran cigar named after Zino Davidoff. The Zino line also includes the Mouton Cadet, made specifically for Baronne de Philippine de Rothschild.

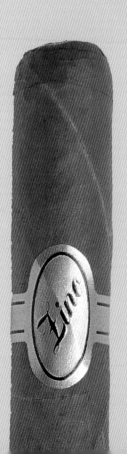

WORLD'S **FLYER** GREATEST

WORLD'S **FLYER** GREATEST

O'SAN

GETTYSBURG COMMANDERS

MEADE.

OUR KITTIES

KYRA

TITLE & DESIGN OWNED BY KYRA CIGAR CO.

JOE MICHL'S
FIFTY LITTLE ORPHANS

KYRA CIGAR CO.
MAKERS.

KYRA

KWALITY
CIGARS

INDEX

Page numbers in **boldface** indicate photo captions.